RESCUE RIDERS

POLICE CARS TO THE RESCUE!

I0794179

BY FRANCES NAGLE

Gareth Stevens
PUBLISHING

Please visit our website, www.garethstevens.com. For a free color catalog of all our high-quality books, call toll free 1-800-542-2595 or fax 1-877-542-2596.

Library of Congress Cataloging-in-Publication Data
Names: Nagle, Frances, 1959- author.
Title: Police cars to the rescue! / Frances Nagle.
Description: New York : Gareth Stevens Publishing, [2023] | Series: Rescue riders | Includes index.
Identifiers: LCCN 2021047107 (print) | LCCN 2021047108 (ebook) | ISBN 9781538278604 (set) | ISBN 9781538278611 (library binding) | ISBN 9781538278598 (paperback) | ISBN 9781538278628 (ebook)
Subjects: LCSH: Police vehicles–Juvenile literature. | Police–Juvenile literature.
Classification: LCC HV7936.V4 N34 2023 (print) | LCC HV7936.V4 (ebook) | DDC 363.2/32–dc23
LC record available at https://lccn.loc.gov/2021047107
LC ebook record available at https://lccn.loc.gov/2021047108

Published in 2023 by
Gareth Stevens Publishing
29 E. 21st Street
New York, NY 10010

Portions of this work were originally authored by B. J. Best and published as *Police Cars*. All new material this edition authored by Frances Nagle.

Copyright © 2023 Gareth Stevens Publishing

Designer: Leslie Taylor
Editor: Kristen Nelson

Photo credits: Cover temp-64GTX/Shutterstock.com; pp. 2-24 (background texture) Pixel Embargo/Shutterstock.com; p. 5 LightField Studios/Shutterstock.com; pp. 7, 9 Photo Spirit/Shutterstock.com; p. 11 kali9/istockphoto.com; p. 13 Andriy Blokhin/Shutterstock.com; p. 15 Kit Leong/Shutterstock.com; p.17 LesPalenik/Shutterstock.com; p.19 Photographee.eu/Shutterstock.com; p. 21 Greg Patton/Shutterstock.com.

All rights reserved. No part of this book may be reproduced in any form without permission in writing from the publisher, except by a reviewer.

Printed in the United States of America

CPSIA compliance information: Batch #CSGS23: For further information contact Gareth Stevens, New York, New York at 1-800-542-2595.

Find us on

CONTENTS

Boldface words appear in the glossary.

Cars Made to Help

It's the job of police officers to help people. They make sure people follow the law. Their cars help them do their jobs! Police cars are made to help police officers get to an **emergency** fast.

A police car may look a lot like a regular car or **SUV**. But, they have been changed for the needs of the police. Police cars have a big **engine**. They have better **brakes** than regular cars.

POLICE

In and On the Car

Police cars have red and blue lights. They have a loud **siren**. When a police car's lights are flashing and its siren is on, cars know to move out of the way. The police car may be on the way to an emergency!

EMERGENCY
911
POLICE

Police officers use **technology** to do their jobs. Police cars have computers and video cameras. They have **radios** so police officers can talk to each other. Police cars have a glass or **mesh** divider inside. People in the backseat can't get to the front.

POLICE
DEPT.

Patrol Car

Police cars are often seen driving around a neighborhood or city. Police officers commonly patrol, or watch over, an area from their car. They also work on roads and highways. Police cars are used to chase down people driving too fast!

METROPOLITAN
POLICE
POLICE
985
MAXIMA

Emergency!

Police cars are emergency **vehicles.** They go to many kinds of emergencies, including fires. A call comes over the radio telling officers what has happened and where it is. The cars closest to the emergency speed there!

1 HOUR
PARKING
9AM - 6PM
ARCADIA
POLICE
57

At a Crash

There has been a car crash! Someone might be hurt. It's time to call the police! When the police car arrives at the crash, some police officers will help people who are hurt. Others direct **traffic** to let other cars drive by safely.

POLICE
CATOUL

At the Scene

When a crime happens, police officers drive to where it happened. This is the crime scene. Police cars help them get there fast! Officers look closely at the scene. They ask questions. They work to figure out what happened.

Colorful Cars

It can be exciting to spot a police car speeding down the road. Years ago, police cars used to be black and white in most places. Today, they can be white with yellow, red, pink, green, or blue! What color are police cars in your city?

STAMFORD
POLICE
CBD CURATORS
30 MINUTE
168
NO PARKING
151-ST

GLOSSARY

brake: the part of a car that slows and stops it

emergency: an unexpected situation that needs quick action

engine: a machine that makes power

mesh: something made from wires with evenly spaced holes that allow air to pass through

radio: a device that is used to send and receive messages by radio

siren: a piece of equipment that produces a loud, high-pitched warning sound

SUV: a large vehicle that is made to be used on rough roads but that is often used on city roads or highways

technology: a machine, piece of equipment, or method created by using science, engineering, and other industries to invent useful tools or to solve problems

traffic: the vehicles moving along a certain road

vehicle: an object that moves people from one place to another

FOR MORE INFORMATION

BOOKS

Johnson, Amy. *Rescue Vehicles.* New York, NY: Windmill Books, 2021.

McDonald, Amy. *Police Cars.* Minneapolis, MN: Bellwether Media Inc., 2022.

WEBSITES

How to Use 911 (for kids)
kidshealth.org/en/kids/911.html

Find out here how to correctly call in an emergency in the United States.

Transportation
www.dkfindout.com/us/transportation/

This website covers all kinds of transportation information.

Publisher's note to educators and parents: Our editors have carefully reviewed these websites to ensure that they are suitable for students. Many websites change frequently, however, and we cannot guarantee that a site's future contents will continue to meet our high standards of quality and educational value. Be advised that students should be closely supervised whenever they access the internet.

INDEX